A Champion's **MEN**tality:
A Blueprint for Kingdom Manhood

Dennis R. Hebert, Jr.

Publishing Co.

ISBN: 978-0-9862040-0-5

DRH Publishing Co.
500 East Hanson Avenue
Hammond, LA 70403
o. 985.429.7545
f . 985.429.7590
www.drhministries.org

A Personal Tribute

To the brave men of the previous generation, who stood committed to serving in the Lord's Church: Your labor was not in vain. I now understand the weight you carried and I applaud your perseverance. More importantly, I accept the challenge of carrying the mantle in champion fashion.

This is my tribute to you!

Forward

When most of us speak of relationship or "fellowship," we're talking about something different than the bond that David and Jonathan enjoyed. We draw invisible lines within our relationships and say, "I will be in relationship with you...as long as it doesn't cost me very much. I will be in relationship with you...as long as it doesn't involve a heavy commitment. I will be in relationship with you...until distance, promotion, or pressing activities draw us apart. I will be in relationship with you...as long as it is convenient...as long as it doesn't embarrass me or cramp my style...as long as it brings me personal pleasure."

We live in a time that says, "You only go around once in a life, so grab all you can. Make a friend, marry a wife, raise a family until it looks like they're beginning to impede your progress, and then kick them to the curb. Write them off. So use anybody you must to get what you want. Then, when they get in your way, kiss them good-bye." That's the kind of world we live in.

God created within us the need for commitment and security in our relationships: in our relationships with God, in our relationships with family, and in our relationships with friends. To the point we remain true to our own commitments, to the point we are willing to sacrifice our own best interests to promote and build in other lives – to that point we find our deepest longings filled.

Civilizations have grown and crumbled away; awesome armies have marched and armies have fallen; once-mighty kings, commanders, and self-proclaimed emperors lie forgotten in ancient mud...but the relationship of Jonathan and David, after 4,000 years, goes on winning hearts and conquering men.

Relationships of this depth and quality are remarkable in themselves; it is all the more remarkable here because the most natural way for Jonathan to treat David would be as a rival, both as a warrior and as a favorite son.

Relationships today have fallen on hard times. We have acquaintances that we pick up from time to time to augment our pleasures or needs, but the kind of spiritual kinship energized by affection and sealed by covenant between David and Jonathan is rare.

Friendship is the least demanding and the least needy of human relationships, but it is also the most necessary for realizing who we are, for becoming ourselves with no strings attached.

Healthy relationships do not restrict our lives; rather, they expand our lives. A friend is one who is attached to another by affection or esteem, a very different circumstance from our family relationships. We have the ability to choose friends, but we can't choose our family. Let's examine the chosen relationship between two friends, Jonathan and David.

These two men were totally committed to each other, vowing that whoever survived and came out on top would protect the other's descendants. Friendship is more than watching games, hanging out, and exchanging Christmas cards and baby pictures. Anyone who cannot discern your worth disqualifies themselves from being your friend.

In Proverbs 18:24, the Bible says, "There is a friend that sticketh closer than a brother." Jonathan and David's story is wonderful example of a great friendship and relationship. But what do you do when storms hit your relationships?

In the book of Job, Chapter 1:18-19, God brings blessings through relationships, but He also allows troubles. The devil thinks that anyone who trusts God without an ulterior motive is a fool. This man, Job, was the greatest of all in the East – spiritually, financially, and domestically. He was a great man. The devil was suspicious of Job's motives. The devil said to God, "He's really not trusting you; you've bought him off! Let me hurt him and you'll see. Let me affect his relationships on every level and we'll see if he still trusts you."

Can you trust God when you are submerged in the suffering of ruined relationships?

In v.13, Job has lost his finances and his herd. In v.13-17, he lost friends. In v.18-19, he lost family and in Chapter 2:4-6, he lost his fitness.

Everyone he was in relationship with questioned him, asking, "What have you been doing wrong? No one innocent suffers like this." Then, Job lost his face (reputation). You lose your reputation when you know you've done nothing wrong and everyone thought you did. However, Job praises God in the midst of his suffering. Can you trust God when you are forsaken by friends, a preacher or someone you are in relationship with?

This book will examine every area and every facet of relationships concerning men. I am so godly proud of my spiritual son, Overseer Dennis R. Hebert, Jr. and I'm standing on tip-toe anticipation waiting to read through the pages of this God-given, vision-manifested book, as I'm sure you are too.

Hats off to you, Man of God! To you the reader, don't just add this book to your dusty bookshelf, make these words live in your heart where the beginning of all healthy relationships grow. Be blessed!

Changing 4 GoOD,

Bishop Darryl S. Brister, PhD
Apostle / Overseer
Beacon Light International Ministries
www.beaconlight.org

Acknowledgments

My seminary professor, Dr. Lisa Hess, writes, in one of her works on ministerial formation, about artisanal theology and this unique method of understanding how God takes us from simple "dough" to a full loaf of bread. As I reflect on all who have helped to form my understanding of purpose and those who have been examples of manhood, up close and from afar, I concur with Dr. Hess' notion of artisanal formation. Truly, there have been so many people, during so many seasons of my life, that have helped shape my worldview of manhood. If I tried to list everyone, I would be certain of excluding someone.

Instead, I thank God for strategically placing "special people" along my path to help enrich my journey. I sincerely appreciate your support and prayers, for without them, I would be grossly lacking for the life's call to which I have been assigned.

However, there are some people that simply cannot go without mention. First and foremost, to my wife and friend for the past two decades, Tranecia: I thank God for you every day. You have been there through every twist and turn of my discovery process. I cannot write about manhood authentically without reflecting on the role you have played in me becoming the man that I am. My three princes, D3, Dylan, and Drake: I pray you guys will always be able to see the footprints I am attempting to leave for you.

To my parents, Dennis Sr. and Doris Hebert: Words are inadequate to describe how grateful I am for your example, both in word and deed. Dad, you have always been my hero and a shining example of what a real man must be and do. I thank you so much for your tireless work ethic, your relentless devotion to God, and your unique way of showing that you love our family more than life.

To Bishop Darryl S. Brister: God connected us at a very critical juncture in my life and used you to birth my identity in God. It is because of your example that a passion rests within me for God's people.

Special thanks to the project dream team, Jeronda Bordenave, Eboney Pegues, and Robin Ware: Your role in this project is invaluable and I bless God for allowing us to work together in ministry. You guys rock!

Thank you to the Beacon Light-Hammond Family. You are the best church on this side of Heaven. I pray that this book enriches your walk with God and provides a clear portrait of biblical manhood.

Contents

A Personal Tribute iii

Forward v

Acknowledgments ix

Introduction... xiii

If— by Rudyard Kipling....................................... xv

Chapter 1 – A Rebound **MEN**tality...................... 1

Chapter 2 – A Praying **MEN**tality...................... 15

Chapter 3 – A Fatherly **MEN**tality..................... 25

Chapter 4 – A Kingdom **MEN**tality..................... 33

Chapter 5 – A Dominion **MEN**tality 41

Chapter 6 – A Persistent **MEN**tality 49

About the Author.. 66

Introduction

On March 8, 2014, one of the greatest mysteries in the field of aviation transpired, one which has continued to confound industry experts. Malaysian Airlines Flight 370 departed from Kuala Lumpur routed to Beijing, China, with 227 souls aboard. Approximately 45 minutes into the flight, the Boeing 777 lost contact with air traffic control and there has been no trace of the missing aircraft since that time. This massive tragedy sent countries from around the world scrambling to send aid and resources to search for the missing plane. Hundreds of millions of dollars and countless human and technical resources have been expended in an effort to find the missing aircraft. It has been labeled a tragedy of incredible proportions.

However, another such tragedy exists within the world that I believe has gone unnoticed by many within the body of Christ. It's the dreadful absence of Kingdom manhood. The roles in which men have traditionally been staples have been abandoned, to the demise of our contemporary culture and succeeding generations. Men in the culture as well as the church have become like the abominable snowman: they haven't been seen, but their fingerprints are everywhere.

The common thing to do, given these facts, is to bash and blame men for their absence and negligence. While the statistics are glaringly discouraging, and often the blame is just, and yes, men must take responsibility for being derelict in their duties, as with all tragedies, there are underlining currents that perpetuate the dilemma we face.

The mentality of our culture has changed drastically and, with that change, many men have lost their identity, purpose, and sense of worth in a changing society. There was a time when men were needed to work, provide, and protect, both in the home and throughout our world. This need supported the male ego and those who were found faithful were considered the heroes or pillars of society.

Today, as many factories stand abandoned in the inner cities as a constant reminder of an economy that has *shifted*, many men have been left behind as *relics* of times past, unneeded for the same roles in which they were once cherished. Men are no longer needed as the *sole* provider in many families; in fact, the statistics are trending towards equality among men and women in education, income earning, and leadership within the culture. The "champion of old" must now be redefined. There must be a new *MENtality* for men so that we can fulfill the *present* need that the world has for strong male leadership.

Our women are waiting; our children are searching; and the world is in need of a fresh **MENtality**.

If—

RUDYARD KIPLING

If you can keep your head when all about you
    Are losing theirs and blaming it on you,
If you can trust yourself when all men doubt you,
    But make allowance for their doubting too;
If you can wait and not be tired by waiting,
    Or being lied about, don't deal in lies,
Or being hated, don't give way to hating,
    And yet don't look too good, nor talk too wise:

If you can dream—and not make dreams your master;
    If you can think—and not make thoughts your aim;
If you can meet with Triumph and Disaster
    And treat those two impostors just the same;
If you can bear to hear the truth you've spoken
    Twisted by knaves to make a trap for fools,
Or watch the things you gave your life to, broken,
    And stoop and build 'em up with worn-out tools:

If you can make one heap of all your winnings
    And risk it on one turn of pitch-and-toss,
And lose, and start again at your beginnings
    And never breathe a word about your loss;
If you can force your heart and nerve and sinew
    To serve your turn long after they are gone,
And so hold on when there is nothing in you
    Except the Will which says to them: 'Hold on!'

If you can talk with crowds and keep your virtue,
    Or walk with Kings—nor lose the common touch,
If neither foes nor loving friends can hurt you,
    If all men count with you, but none too much;
If you can fill the unforgiving minute
    With sixty seconds' worth of distance run,
Yours is the Earth and everything that's in it,
    And—which is more—you'll be a Man, my son!

Chapter 1

A Rebound **MEN**tality

God's Going to Do It Again

Exodus 2:15 NKJV

[15] *When Pharaoh heard of this matter, he sought to kill Moses.*
But Moses fled from the face of Pharaoh and dwelt in the land of
Midian; and he sat down by a well.

William Shakespeare, a noted British poet and playwright, said that there are "sermons in stones" and those of us who have eyes of faith can see God in the most miniscule matters of life. The voice of God cannot be restricted to what we hear audibly, for God can direct us through mundane daily encounters. I found this to be true one day as I was with our youth basketball team. Basketball is a means through which I have been able to influence the lives of young men and impart principles that will impact them far beyond the court.

It's not just recreation for me; it is actually ministry. I am paying forward to the next generation what so many coaches and men in the neighborhood did for me as a youth. As I pour into the life of these young fourth-, fifth-, and sixth-graders, I see them as historymakers in the making. As I coach them, God often speaks to me as I attempt to instruct the team.

Often in basketball practice, we will run a drill designed to teach positioning and technique for rebounding. On this one day, these words of Shakespeare rang in my spirit as I saw that there are correlations between "rebounding" in the game of basketball and rebounding in the game of life. "Rebounding" means that an attempt was taken and failed. A shot was attempted and missed, and a rebound becomes necessary.

Invariably in the game of basketball, and even in the game of life, there will be well-intentioned attempts that we will make as men, fathers, and yes, even as Christians, that will fail. Failing is unavoidable, but rebounding is an option. There has never been a player who has played the game of basketball, who never missed a shot. If we are honest and observant, we must admit there is evidence of "missed shots" all around us. Whether it's a business venture that "went south" or inconsistent morals that have led to the destruction of the family, we all can point at "missed shots."

Again, there has never lived a man upon the earth who has not experienced seasons of failure. In fact, if you really want to learn to be a champion in life, the first lesson is learning how to lose. It's the scars from these lessons that serve as reminders and cause us to stand so confidently during seasons of triumph. In life, there is no such thing as a "perfect season." In fact, champions are born out of the disgust and disappointment of failure.

There are several reasons why our attempts may fail, both in basketball and in life. First of all, your perspective could be off. Perhaps you misjudged the goal and the power behind the attempt may have been too hard, too short, or too long. Your perspective of the goal that you were trying to reach was "off." A distorted perspective can have a dangerous effect on life outcomes because perspective shapes reality. When perspective is off, we can mistake friends as enemies and enemies as friends.

It is difficult at best to succeed without seeing clearly. The devil has done a great deception job on most men through shifting our values from things that are lasting to things that are temporary. Consequently, we tend to spend more of our time, energy, and money on things that will not provide lasting value in our lives. The pursuit of success without the foundation and temperament of spiritual direction is such a case.

Another reason that you may miss a shot or fail at an attempt is because somebody was "in your face." Your view of the target was off because you were distracted. While trying to succeed at a particular goal, someone had his hand in your face. The devil loves to use weapons of "mass distraction." Broken focus is often the demise of so many great feats. I have noticed this happens often at preaching events. There are times when we say, "Wow, that man or woman of God was anointed today!" However, what I have come to realize is that the anointing of God doesn't just rest at *some* times and not at other times. More often, it's a matter of the preacher's focus during preparation. If the devil can get your focus, then he can minimize your effectiveness.

There are brothers who can identify with the fact that they wasted golden opportunities because something or someone broke their focus. I can look back at moments in my life, especially when I was in college, that I knew I could have performed better, but there were so many *other* things that were "in my face" that distracted me from peak performance.

In basketball, still, there is the reality that someone may have fouled you and caused you to fail. When a foul is called, it means someone handled or touched you illegally. You could have had this misfortune; however, you don't quit the game because you were fouled and, even if the referee didn't make the proper call, you don't leave the court and take off your jersey because you were fouled. You simply missed the shot!

As harsh and unfair as that may sound, champions must understand that excuses are not accepted. Fatherless, poor education, abuse, and/or neglect can no longer be excuses for you to stay stuck in a failed situation. There are others who have succeeded despite what someone did or didn't do for them. The devil loves to put folk "in your face" to discourage, distract, or deceive you into thinking that you can't succeed because of what happened to you. The devil is a liar!

Regardless of what caused you to fail, the revelation from the game of basketball is that we must have a "rebound mentality," a comeback spirit. In running our rebounding drills, we teach three things: bend your knees, box out, and jump off the floor. These are the rules for the rebound. I encourage you to get the revelation as you read this. First, bend your knees in prayer; it's where every great comeback starts. Do you know that it's impossible to jump without bending your knees first? It's impossible for you to rebound after a miss if you don't bend at the knees first.

"Praying men" have become something that we only *read about* in the Bible. I remember, when growing up in my church, we had some strong women who could pray, but there were men who could call down fire from heaven as well. Every man should have a vibrant prayer life because it speaks to his humility and submission to God as his Source. Whatever you do without prayer, you do without God!

"Boxing out" is fundamental, and those who learn this art will always maintain their focus. To "box out" means to "push out" or "keep away" the competition. We must be careful to box out all of the distractions that the devil sends. Due to your champion pedigree, you will always have those who are sent to compete for your focus, loyalty, and love with deceptive intentions. In fact, these may be your peers and possibly family members who may come to persuade you to "keep it real." The problem is that they are doing nothing to help advance your purpose or push you closer to God. In order to get better, you have to box out; there is no way around it.

I know, firsthand, the ridicule that comes when you begin to box out; however, the greatest deliverance that we can ever experience is when we are *delivered* from people's opinions of us. We must box out those who carry negativity, those who remind us of our failures, and who refuse to celebrate who we are becoming.

The final rule for the rebound is, jump off the floor. It's very difficult to get a rebound if you stay planted on the floor. Whatever you do, *don't sit in your setback*. Jump off the floor! Use that failed experience as a springboard to propel you into your next season. It's so easy and comfortable to stay planted on the floor and bemoan the circumstance. I have dealt with the depression of disappointments, and even embarrassment; however, progress is never made when we stay on the floor.

During one of the darkest seasons of my life, a close friend came to encourage me and he said, "Dennis, whatever you do, keep it moving because when you stay still, you become an easy target for the devil." Whatever happened has happened, but don't let the devil keep you down. Keep it moving because it's hard to hit a moving target.

Whatever that failed attempt is in your life, I hear God telling you to jump off the floor. Get up and declare that you are not defeated, but *determined* to make your *next* move your *best* move. That's the mark of a winner!

My pastor would always say that in the church, we are guilty of "shooting the wounded." Those who come in failed and fallen in life are painted as a picture of a "merciless God" and we leave them on the floor of life. It has been God's reputation throughout Scripture to grant grace in times of need. Scripture shows many who have triumphed after tragedy. God is able to catch you on the rebound! You need to know, understand, and believe that.

The Bible is not necessarily a "history book." Whenever a history book is written, it is usually authored by a "victor." The victorious author may leave out certain parts of the story so that the appearance of being victorious continues throughout the pages. Rather than being a history book, the Bible is a book of destiny, written from Divine Inspiration. Through related dispensations, the Bible was written. If it had been engineered by man, Abraham would have left out the part of his story about Hagar; Samson would have left out Delilah, and David would have left out Bathsheba. Certainly there are aspects of our history that may be bad, or even ugly, but your failures are part of your story and not the *totality* of your story. Even Moses, who God anointed and appointed to lead the children of Israel out of Egyptian captivity, became one of the most revered persons in Jewish history. He authored the first five books of the Jewish Bible, the Pentateuch, yet Moses needed a rebound. We all can glean something from his life that can be applicable to our consideration of purpose and destiny. When you find yourself in situations as Moses found himself, God wants you to know that *you*, too, can make a rebound.

The truth of Moses' whole story is that he was born during the reign of an insecure king. Pharaoh was living in the fear that he might be taken down by a nation that was *not* Egyptian. They had enslaved and persecuted them; thus, they had every right, if not the intention or the capacity, to rebel against him. He feared the rise of a God-fearing Hebrew man. The "spirit of Pharaoh" is alive and well today because men who are willing to stand up regardless of the consequences are still a threat to the powers of darkness.

Satan operates the same way as Pharaoh did. He has a fear that there will be those who will rise up and tear down his kingdom. This is particularly true in places where black boys and men reside in large numbers. He might not have an overt law that discriminates against strong men, but he operates covertly. The welfare system is set up to leave men out; the justice system is unfavorable to black men; and sadly, even the religious system tends to exclude ministry to transform men.

One cannot help but see the similarities that exist between the Hebrews and African Americans. There are inequities in the penalties for selling cocaine versus crack. In education, the facilities and instructors for black schoolchildren are inferior to those of their white counterparts. That prison terms have been established with the longevity to make sure black men don't return to the streets, even if they become "rehabilitated," is obvious. This is precisely the reason that there are more black men in prison cells than in classes on college campuses.

The devil's system applauds black men snorting, drinking, and dancing all day because if they discover who they really are, they will discover who they are not. That will have the result of tearing down everything that makes them appear "the fool."

In doing some research on Moses, I became curious about the background of his father. All I could derive is that he was from the tribe of Levi. By implication and history, I knew that there was strength in the worship of the Levites and there was a deep ritualistic order embedded in the character of that tribe.

History reveals that the raging fears of Pharaoh caused him to declare that male babies be killed. By eliminating male children,

Pharaoh would have minimized the threat to his sovereignty. Moses' mother hid her child and would not let him become part of the genocide that was going on in the streets. I'm sure that there are some men who thought they had the meanest mother in the world when, in fact, she was "hiding" them from death in the streets. She didn't want to see her son hanging out in the streets because of the imminent dangers that her son could not see.

Looking back at those ingenious strategies that the mothers employed, there are brothers who can appreciate it now. There is no telling where some of us would be today had we not been ordered to be home before the street lights lit up. We cannot ignore the fact that the devil wants to kill our boys, and there are some "new-day mothers" who need to grasp on to Grandma's awareness and keep their sons in the house.

It is equally important that the text says that Moses' mother kept him in the house "until she could no longer hide him." Mothers have to be careful that the protection or the covering that is given is not overprotection. The need to protect your sons does not suggest that you have to turn them into "momma's boys." At a certain point, you must release them. The mother of Moses placed him in a basket that would float him in the river. That act, in and of itself, was not an act of desperation on her part; it was a pronouncement that God would take care of him.

I suspect that there are those women who have kept their children so close that even God can't get to them. This arrests their development and skews their perspective of what manhood really means. Mothers should never confuse their sons with their husbands. Keep your husband close, but release your son so that he can be what God would have him become. Every boy has to be released at some point (unless you are going to "neuter" him).

Spiritually, Moses' mother relinquished her job as provider and picked up the role of "intercessor." She could do more with her prayers to God on her knees than she could hiding him continuously in the house. Get that boy out of the house!

The story evolves to the point that her son, floating in the river, is observed by the daughter of Pharaoh while she was bathing. I submit to you that while her son was floating, *she* was praying. Though the son was no longer hidden from danger at home with her, she had a blessed assurance of his safety because of her praying.

The move of God is so evident in this whole story. Pharaoh's daughter admired the child and her servant noted that, if she took the child, someone would have to be found to take care of it. It was no coincidence that the mother of Moses was employed, if not engaged, to take care of *her own* child. Both of them were together again in the same household that had declared resentment to the mother and death to the child. That which the devil meant to destroy can end up delivering you.

Prior to this time, Moses was condemned to death, but in his changed circumstances, he had the best that was available. Both he and his mother now resided in the King's palace. He had moved from a floating crib basket to the best bed in the house. Contemporarily speaking, he was no longer subject to miseducation in the public schools; he was in a private academy. He had been unceremoniously moved to the other side of the tracks. He was exposed to the best of everything because he had a mama that prayed. It may be old-fashioned to say it, but there is a sweet relief in knowing that God will make a way somehow.

While his mother could not dismiss the blessings that they had received in the house of Pharaoh, she had a moral and cultural obligation to remind Moses of the God-given legacy that he had. He could not be allowed to forget that he was Hebrew, not Egyptian.

This became important later in his life when he was confronted with making a decision that crossed his cultural line of demarcation.

Observing two separate incidents of men fighting – one Egyptian and the other Hebrew – Moses interceded and killed the Egyptian. Perhaps he could have exercised more restraint or used his position and status as a part of the royal family in a more acceptable manner, but he killed. He looked around to see who had seen him and chose to bury the man in the sand. At that point, he became a fugitive. The killing was a result of a sympathetic conflict and not something that he had premeditated. He tried to hide what he had done, which is more than some folk try to do, those who could care less who know what they did. He killed a man and buried him in the sand. Brothers, if we would be honest, that's what we do when we mess up: we go into cover-up mode.

In the second incident of violent encounter, one of the protagonists asked Moses whether he was going to do to them what he had done to the Egyptian. We can imagine the sense of shock in Moses because he thought he had been successful in hiding the fact that he had killed the Egyptian. The question then becomes, who told?

Perhaps the person who made it known to him was the one who Moses tried to help in the fight. That's the only explanation that appears obvious. I have concluded that you have to be careful who you help or to whom you "do dirt" with, because they can become a burden to you later. They will tell it!

There is a principle that can be seen in the behavior of both Moses and his dilemma. There is little doubt that the mother of Moses had taught him that no man can rise above the condition of his people. Moses was no longer seen as a son of Pharaoh, but as an ungrateful Hebrew who took advantage of his position in Pharaoh's house.

Constructing a building can take a long time, sometimes years. The pre-construction work requirement alone can take months, if not years, to complete before the building construction even begins. In total, it can take 2–3 years from architectural conception to completion for a building to be constructed. Interestingly, while it takes years to construct a building, it can only take a few minutes for demolition. One click of a button, and what took years to plan and construct can become rubble in a matter of minutes. Moses had built his reputation and life over a period of forty years, but now this *one* mistake was about to cause everything to come tumbling down.

Man, do you see why we should be prayerful and committed to God? Because one wrong move and everything we have given our lives for can come tumbling down. Moses was forced to think about what could have been, if he had not made that one bad decision. He was on the backside of the desert and had given up on himself, but God had not given up on him. All he needed was a fresh encounter with God to turn his life around.

The subsequent incidental encounter with God via the burning bush was Moses' defining moment. He needed an encounter with God. The bush-burning in the narrative was important because it represented a moment of worship that was not expected by Moses in his moment of deep depression. You may be one fresh encounter away from making a comeback.

There is something about a man who is unafraid to lift his hands in worship. I remember when God arrested me and made it clear that I should never come into his Presence trying to look all high and mighty. First and foremost, God reminded me that I didn't *deserve* to be in His Presence. I had to come to the point that I realized that I wanted some fire in my life and my hands went up in total adoration to God, as antennas seeking a communicative frequency with heaven.

It was on Sinai in the Presence of God that Moses was told to remove his shoes. He was in the Presence of God, but the *place* that he was in was also holy. It was holy because of the Presence of God. The removal of his shoes – being barefoot before the Lord – was a sign of humility, surrender, and faith. Therein lies the problem with some men – they don't know how or they refuse to be "barefoot before God." You may take it as a sign of weakness, even vulnerability, but the Bible clearly says that every knee shall bow and every tongue shall confess that Jesus Christ is Lord. Eventually, you are going to have to come to the reality that our spiritual journey is made "barefooted."

Notice that God never instructed Moses to put his shoes back on. This indicates that we are to live our lives by faith and that God will order every step and protect us from destruction.

Prior to this event, there is no record of the religious affiliation or spiritual formation of Moses. There is nothing to indicate that he ever prayed. We know about the prayers of his mother, but we have no evidence of any conversation that Moses had with God before this juncture in his life. This suggests that, like Moses, many men have been living off the prayers of their mothers, grandmothers, and "church mothers." Moses had never humbled himself to the point of becoming submissive before God and it was the prayers of his mother that helped to keep him covered..

Perhaps because of Moses' privileged position in growing up in Pharaoh's house, he became the captain of his own soul and master of his own fate. It is so easy for us to get distracted in our achievements and pursuits and not recognize that there is an invisible God behind the scenes ordering our affairs and keeping close watch over our lives. God brought Moses to a place in his life where he realized that he could no longer be dependent on the prayers of his mother, but he would have to know God for himself.

Brothers, there must come a time when we refuse to be spiritual "momma's boys." God will allow trials in our lives, not to punish us, but to bring us closer to Him.

God made it clear that it would be only in this context of encounter with Him that Moses could have a rebound. He had to know that it was going to be impossible to make a rebound if he was standing straight up. It couldn't be done! He was going to have to humble himself before God. The way to go up is to come down! Humility allows you to "reload" for your rebound. Humbling yourself before God always leads to elevation.

"Shoes off" is a sign of commitment, trust, and more importantly, vulnerability before God. There are very few areas where men find it acceptable to be vulnerable. We will do everything possible to hide our frailties. You will find it almost impossible to make a true commitment to anything until it makes you uncomfortable. Anyone can stand in a place when everything is in line and there is no evidence of obstacles or resistance, but can you stand when things get uncomfortable and you really don't know how they are going to turn out? A real man has to know that he can't run every time his foot gets stuck or things don't look like they are working out. The question is whether he is committed to stand. Is he committed before God? Real faith is not knowing that everything is going to turn out OK; it's being OK with how things turn out and knowing that you will prevail.

I submit that there is a shortage of men who are truly committed to something. I'm talking about something that is bigger than themselves. Our present mentality is supported by a culture that teaches us to focus on self and self alone. However, we stand the tallest when we are bending over helping someone else to come up. Just because your current position is *uncomfortable* doesn't mean it's *unbearable*. It takes a crucified man to live a life for a crucified

Christ. It's time to ManUp and shift our mentality. This next season is going to be your best season. Tell the devil, "I'm bouncing back!"

Chapter 2

A Praying **MEN**tality

Winning the Battle on Your Knees

In my pastoral role, I have to counsel couples during pre-marital sessions. It's always interesting to see how naïve many of them are as they sit on the thick leather couch in my office in obvious pre-marital bliss. When we begin to discuss practical and biblical ways to have a strong and enduring life with one another, I always ask them the question, "How many married friends do you have?" While the answers vary, the principle behind the question is that which I'm ultimately aiming for.

We cannot win battles in isolation. Whenever the devil can cause us to become isolated, that is when he can attack our minds and disorient our spiritual compass. Thus, it's always good to know that you have others in the battle with you and that you are not fighting a battle that no one else has ever fought before.

We are all involved in some level of spiritual warfare because everything that we come against has a spiritual origin. Spiritually speaking, the waged battle is in the theater of our prayer lives, so the armor of God is needed in order for us to be victorious. If we are not properly covered, our prayers won't avail because of the influence that the enemy exerts on uncovered believers.

If there is anything that gives the devil a headache, it's when a man prays. Brothers, when we pray, it is the height of spiritual warfare and it provides a covering for our lives. We cannot afford to fight our battles simply from a natural standpoint. Natural weapons produce natural results, but spiritual weapons can produce spiritual results. To win and to win every time, we must learn to fight our battles on our knees.

"We fight with weapons that are different from those the world uses. Our weapons have power from God that can destroy the enemy's strong places. We destroy people's arguments." II Corinthians 10:4 NCV

There is a real enemy faced by all of us. If you are not at the point in your spiritual walk where you believe in spiritual warfare, you are already defeated. The spirit realm is more real than the natural realm. What we neglect in the spirit will manifest itself in the natural. The devil's influence on the uncovered believer causes him to doubt and second-guess God and wonder if his prayers are really availing.

It causes us to be forgetful concerning God's Word and His Promises, and eventually the devil defeats us through the fiery darts that he launches against our lives.

The level of our spiritual development will never rise any higher than the level of our prayer life.

There is a direct connection between your peace, joy, and Godly confidence and your prayer life. How you handle the trials and adversities of your life is a litmus test of your level of spirituality.

I can reflect on so many seasons of prayerlessness in my life and the results spoke for themselves. Truly, if there is prayer, there is power and where there is prayerlessness, there is confusion, discord, and the probability of going astray. The enemy defeats many of us because Satan causes us to sit on the sideline, spiritually, and not engage God through prayerful dialogue. He exerts his influence on us to change our priority of praying. What can be more important to a believer in God than daily prayer? The battle for the blessings and victory that God wants us to have is fought on our knees. We win on our knees!

Prayerlessness Makes Us Powerless

Many brothers don't pray because they are simply ignorant of the *benefits* of prayer. Developing a prayer life is one of the most beneficial habits you could ever begin. There is an assurance that God gives to us when we call; He answers and reveals to us what we should do. This is what happens in prayer. God responds and shows us what we are supposed to do. Note, if you would, that God *won't* do it for us, but He will show us the great things that *we* should do.

> "Call to me and I will answer you. I'll tell you marvelous and wondrous things that you could never figure out on your own." Jeremiah. 33:3 MSG

There is yet another reason that many neglect prayer: It is because they are overcome by habitual sin. Yes, sin displeases God, but sin should never drive us away from talking with God. It is when we find ourselves the most distant that we really need prayer the most. Again, the devil's work is most effective if he can keep distance between a man and his Creator. God knows *all* of our sins, and yet He is never surprised by any of them! The Bible says that He remembers that we are only dust.

"For He Himself knows our frame; He is mindful that we are but dust."
Psalm 103:14 NKJV

Therefore, if we find ourselves in any form of sin, we shouldn't neglect prayer. We should pray even more for God to restore and to release forgiveness over our lives. Too often in the church we present a merciless God who is out to destroy us at even the slightest mistake. This could not be further from the truth. I know firsthand how the devil, and even those who work for him, can cast condemnation upon us to make us feel so unworthy to be connected to God. In many regards, the Body of Christ has been guilty of "shooting the wounded." When hurting people, whether they are believers or unbelievers, present with sin problems, we shun them or "make a motion" that they are excommunicated, when in truth they need the Love of God to restore them. The devil will always shout out our mistakes while whispering our accomplishments. Though God will never condemn us, the Holy Spirit will convict us.

"Condemnation" and "conviction" sound alike, but there is a drastic difference between these two words. Condemnation leaves you paralyzed and ashamed. Conviction, however, always leads to repentance. I thank God that He loves me enough to have the Holy Spirit convict me and lead me back to repentance in prayer. God uses all aspects of our living to pull us closer to Him. Even those aspects of our lives that we are ashamed and embarrassed about, God wants to use that to draw us closer. One of God's attributes is that He is most gracious and merciful. God has both the grace to forgive our sin(s) and the power to deliver us out of any sin; but we must Man Up prayed up.

Overconfident in Your Own Ability

The example of a champion can be seen in the life and ministry of Jesus. There are certain examples concerning the life of Jesus that are "teaching moments" for us in our walk with God. Jesus' entire life was bathed in prayer. This is how he was able to live victoriously in a Satanic world. He was able to conquer all that came against him because he stayed in connection with God through prayer. The power is in "the connection," brothers. We can never get overconfident in our power, our wisdom, or our understanding that we neglect the power of connecting with our Creator. Now if Jesus, the Savior of the world, had to pray daily, you must know that you and I will have to consistently pray as well.

Jesus won because He fought His battles on his knees. He took advantage of His heavenly resources. That's what His life of prayer should teach all of us: we have resources that we are *not* using. We are losing battles because we refuse to draw on the power that God has given us through prayer.

Prayer is designed for us to speak to God and for God to speak to us. Please know that God still speaks today, but He speaks when we seek Him through prayer. God wants to talk to you; He is ready to show you things you have not yet seen and grant you direction to live the victorious life.

Six Keys to Producing a Prosperous Prayer-life.

1. Pray when you are busy.

Whether you realize it or not, we all have priorities in life. The question is, who sets your priorities? Do you set them or do others determine your priorities? Whenever you resort to saying that you are too busy to pray, you have determined prayer's priority.

All of us live busy lives and all of us face crazy schedules and appointments that we have to meet; so did Jesus. Despite His dealing and traveling, he set time for prayer.

2. Pray when you are tired.

Jesus had a lifestyle of prayer, not a prayer life built out of convenience and emotionalism. He understood the importance of prayer and that, even when we are physically tired, we still need to seek God.

We must be very careful when we get too tired. The devil can take advantage of us when we are tired. Jesus taught us through His life's ministry that even when you are tired, you should seek God through prayer.

Creating a prayer life is one built upon a habit of doing something, no matter what. One can tell what you are committed to by what you do when you are tired.

It's during those tired moments and tired seasons that we should seek God for rest, for refreshing, etc.

3. Pray when you need to make a decision.

In the selection of those who would be the closest to Him in His life's work, Jesus prayed. He had several people from whom he could choose; He had over 70 disciples, but those whom He would be the closest with, for them He prayed.

Prayer takes the pressure out of making tough decisions. When we seek God, He gives us the direction and the strength to make tough decisions, especially those concerning destiny. There have been times when I was facing hard choices in my life and I didn't have the words to speak or couldn't discern when was the right time. It was when I prayed that God orchestrated everything to enable the conversation to be had and the decision to easy.

You should never make a life-altering decision without praying to hear God's voice. Many of us are guilty of voicing our concerns when we should be hearing the voice of God. We cannot allow the devil to lead us into making decisions without first praying. When we do, we are bound to miss something that our eyes cannot see.

4. Pray when you face trials.

Probably the most difficult time to pray, for all believers, is when you are bombarded with trials. This is when prayer in the Spirit avails much. That is the time when we go to God, even when we are hurting too badly to come up with the right words to say.

The Spirit will make the utterance, but it's on us to seek Him. Jesus was acquainted with trouble and with trials; He stayed in trouble! People continuously misunderstood Him and tried to set Him up; but the reason He remained so cool was that He had a connection to God. He had the confidence in knowing God during His time of trials.

There are demons that we have to face that will only be driven out by prayer and supplement. Tormenting and evil spirits will come upon us and we must engage in prayer to defeat them.

5. Pray to know the Father's Will.

Not every battle that presents itself is a battle that we are supposed to fight. There are some battles that God will give us the anointing to win and others He wants us to completely stay away from. This is why we must have a praying mentality: to avoid battles that were never meant for us to engage in.

You never want to be engaged in any project that is costing you time, labor, and resources and *not* be in the Will of God. Until we die, we all will be fighting some kind of battle. Therefore, make sure you save your resources for battles that matter. We all must know God's Will for our lives. We have purpose and fulfillment when we are walking in His Will. It is not what others want for me or even what I may desire; it's God's will that's the best option. Sometimes we don't know what's in us and what God has equipped us with, but when we seek God's Will, he directs us.

Praying for His Will sometimes makes you uncomfortable because God will show you when you are *not* operating in His Will and His Plan for you. He will check you about your attitude, the way you treat others, or how you handled someone in a conversation.

6. Pray for others.

When we really develop a prosperous prayer life, we will see the need to intercede for others. In fact, we will begin seeking out people for whom to pray.

Praying for others does not require you to know the specifics in their lives, and when God is leading you to pray for others, He will always give us the unction to release prayer in certain areas.

Your prayer life should not be for selfish purposes only. There are times when you should pray for people who can't do anything for you and whom you may even dislike. God will put us in the position to pray for those who we may not know personally, but cover them during trials or encourage them through prayer. To be an effective intercessor, we must be comfortable being led of the Sprit in prayer.

Every brother must have some "knee-time" to keep his sanity and to prosper his spirit. There is no way that you can win alone, but every time you pray, victory is yours.

Chapter 3

A Fatherly **MEN**tality

It's Worth the Sacrifice!

1 Corinthians 4:15 NKJV

*"For though you have had ten thousand instructors
(boy leaders)...you have not had many fathers..."*

Meeting the responsibilities of fatherhood is a very demanding task, one for which most brothers are ill-equipped because fathers are conspicuously missing in our culture. It is safe to say that these are not good days for fathers and the times in which we live are not very friendly to fathers. We live in a society that promotes fatherlessness via social benefits and a plethora of other institutional biases, including the church.

It is a daunting observation and it speaks to the generations of children yet unborn. The American family is living under a systemic curse of fatherlessness. It is a cultural curse and the traces of it are seen in every sector of society.

Everywhere we turn in our world, the common pervasive ills of fatherlessness are screaming at us in dramatic fashion. Sixty-three percent of children who commit suicide have not experienced the love of their father. Eighty percent of all rapists never had a father *in* his life. Seventy-eight percent of children described as delinquents in state detention had no father figure in their lives. The curse is screaming at us. Ninety percent of black prisoners have had no father in their lives. It is clear indication of a generation living in a cursed culture.

Children, particularly young men, have mothers who have loved them, but they have never experienced a father's love, guidance or mentoring. I salute the sisters who have had to play both roles, and many have done so successfully, but there is no equivalent to a father's love and consistent presence in a young child's life. I give full commendation to those who qualify in this category because to be a father means that you must endure certain discomforts so that your children will be blessed. It's a role of constant sacrifice and low appreciation, but is so necessary to the formation of real manhood.

There is a difference between being loved by a mother and being loved by a father. A mother cuddles, coddles, and comforts. She makes sure that her baby feels good in many regards.

A father's love is one that corrects, makes the child conform, and gives instructions, and that is totally different from a mother's love. Men are always harder on their sons because they are replicating themselves. They can see things in them that were once in themselves.

When there aren't enough strong fathers in the culture, it sets the succeeding generation of families up for failure. Women will have to assume roles that they can do, but shouldn't have to do. Children are forced to find father figures in people who aren't qualified or, many times, even interested in being father figures. Relationally, because a true father or man is not present in the culture, it appears that we are driving a generation of women into being single for life, or perhaps into lesbianism, having only been loved by their mothers but never having known a man's love because there are so few qualified men to seriously consider. They have been mothered but have never been loved by a father. In every regard, fathers help society go farther by passing on to their children their wisdom, and instilling confidence and family pride.

I remember having some problems at home early on in my marriage and I left home in a rage. I went to my father's office so that we could talk about it. He began to counsel me, and when he was through hearing me out and sharing his advice, he told me to go right back home because I couldn't stay with him. He had said all that he needed to say and the only thing left was for me to go home and work it out. He taught me that as a man, you can't run from your issues. Sometimes when it's hot in the kitchen, you don't run and leave – you raise a window and cool the kitchen off. If it had been my mother, she would have told me to come home and stay with them for a while until things got better. That is the difference in the two kinds of love.

Furthermore, my children are depending on me to get it together and work it out. The temporary discomfort was overshadowed by the long-term responsibility I had to my children and my wife and those who look to me as an example. Again, father is one who sees farther! He must see farther than the pain, farther than discomfort, farther than the disagreement, and see the joy that comes after one has endured. Just like Jesus, every real man will have a cross to carry. As we successfully carry our crosses, something greater will live as a result.

Jesus' sacrifice speaks to us all about the blessing on the other side of sacrifice. His sacrifice was shameful and seemingly unfruitful during his present struggle. I thank God that Jesus' mentality was bigger than just his personal comfort and happiness. It's because of this sacrifice that so many others can live in eternity. That word, "sacrifice," means that something has to die so that something greater can live. When fathers sacrifice, we allow something greater than us and more lasting than us to live.

Heb. 12:2 NKJV

2 Looking unto Jesus, the author and finisher of our faith, who for the joy that was set before Him endured the cross, despising the shame, and has sat down at the right hand of the throne of God.

It's Time to Grow Up

There was a lesson learned for me: society will not coddle you, for it takes no prisoners. When my dad dropped me off at college for the first time, he gave me a hundred dollars and told me not to call him for money until the next month. He charged me with the responsibility of managing my money until the next month came. I had never had to manage my money before, for I was only seventeen years old at the time. Quickly I learned to have a long-term mentality in order to budget my needs over my wants. Little did I know my father was maturing my mentality with a crash course in reality. These are skills that young man should glean from his father, but when the father is absent, oftentimes these lessons go untaught, to the detriment of the sons.

This is a social stigma, but it's not a social problem. It cannot be solved simply with therapy or consultation. Having a couch session with a psychiatrist or psychologist will not provide long-term and comprehensive solutions to this dilemma. It is a problem where men and women are missing a key ingredient in their lives that could provide balance. They're missing it!

In the Book of Malachi, we have a book of warnings. He shares the spiritual ramifications that come upon a culture when they leave the teachings of God. When the presence of the Lord is active in your life, you are blessed, no doubt about it. Blessings are not what you have externally, but what is on the inside. You can lose everything you have and still be blessed. When you have the blessing, no devil in hell can take it from you. Conversely, to be cursed is the actions that you take that prevent God from moving in your life. Make sure that there is no reckless disregard for God in your life, for that's when the curse comes in. God warned the people about remembering to honor God (Malachi 1:6). He warned them about letting honor to God fail in their lives.

He warned the parents about honoring their commitments to their children. The curse is from a spiritual problem and it demanded a spiritual remedy. The seed of the father is transferred to the child. In the sequence of blessings from Abraham, Isaac, and Jacob, the transfer agent was obvious; it was the father who transferred the blessing onto the son. It is no surprise, then, that Satan tries to interrupt fathers from transferring the blessings by disconnecting them from God first and then from their family second. Moreover, without that transfer, only a curse remains. We have a society that is seeing the *lack* of a father's blessing.

A generation is searching for "daddy's blessing" in all the wrong places. You can see them on every corner, searching for daddy's blessings. When there is no father's blessing, Satan comes and suggests the frame of your future. When a father speaks blessings over his household, there is a surety for the future. There is a spiritual inheritance connected to the father, for the blessing is in the transfer. A mother has to be careful not to adopt the attitude that because the child's father has not done what he was supposed to do by her, he then becomes ineligible to see or to have relationships with his children. This is dangerous, not just for the children, but for the woman because she makes herself the obstacle that prevents the father from doing that which he was ordained by God to do. The future of that child is dependent upon his receiving the blessing!

It is a hard thing to be something that you have never seen. The Book of Ezekiel declares that the fathers will eat the sour grapes, but the children will suffer from it. In other words, the fathers will make the bad decision, but the children will reap the punishment. It's time to change our mentality and Man Up! There is a responsibility on men for their children that's not on women, and there has to be a mentality shift to know that it's worth the sacrifice to secure our sons' and our daughters' future.

How do we reverse the curse? The word tells us emphatically, by remembering the Law of Moses. The remedy is remembering the Lord! You have to be able to remember what God promised. When things are not going well in the family, remember the Lord. When you see the curse setting in, remember the Lord! What we see happening in the streets clearly shows that someone has forgotten the Lord. That's why it is important for a father to accompany their children to church and not send them alone, for a father to help check homework, to be present at the ball games and not to become disinterested in matters concerning the child. Fathers are not those who are merely present – fathers function in the child's life.

God wants men to repent, which means to turn around. You're going in the wrong direction, but if you can remember the Lord, you can return and come back to God. He never shuts the door to a son that is returning home, no matter what. There is an announcement that a "sign" will be seen and recognized that the time has come for a shift in mentality. It a spiritual sign. It's not the actual return of Christ; it is the announcement that Christ *will* return. That announcement, the Bible says, will turn the hearts of men back to God and back to their family. A social agency should not have to tell you how much you need to give a month to take care of your children. When the shift comes, a man will gladly do more than expected. There ought to be the acceptance that if you brought them into the world, you have an obligation, and no one needs to remind you of that. God is going to take some selfish brothers, consumed with themselves, and turn them around to save a generation. The hearts of the fathers will be turned back to their children, and a generation that is out of control and out of touch with God will be saved.

There is a story that is told about hunters who had come in to kill bull elephants for their ivory. Due to all the mature elephants being killed, the younger, immature elephants were left out of control. They were knocking over trees and ravaging the landside. The decision was made to fly in some mature male elephants and put them into the herds. They noticed that when the mature elephants got into the herd, they would raise their trunk and make loud noises so as to establish some authority and order. As the younger bulls saw what was happening, they began to get in line and order was restored. Notice order was restored when the older, mature elephants took charge in the midst of the young bulls. They raised their trunk and began to establish order.

That's what needs to happen among young men in our culture today. We need to have men who are willing to get in the midst of the young boys and girls and show them the need for order and responsibility. It will take the raising of our trunks and the lifting of our voices and the sacrificing of our personal desires, but it's well worth the sacrifice. Mature men need to bring the herd of young men who are on the streets or who have not lifted their trousers, who are not educating themselves, to understand that there is a place for order. This job is not for the selfish at heart; it's for champions who have a father's mentality.

Chapter 4

A Kingdom **MEN**tality:

The Mission to Men

I Timothy 3:14 NKJV

[14] These things I write to you, though I hope to come to you shortly; [15] but if I am delayed, I write so that you may know how you ought to conduct yourself in the house of God, which is the church of the living God, the pillar and ground of the truth.

When we consider the Mission of Jesus, He came to save those who were lost. Every year thousands of Christian missionaries travel abroad to remote, impoverished areas of the world to minister the gospel of salvation. Often placing themselves in harm's way, these missionaries are committed to taking the gospel to every corner of the earth. Many forsake family and personal comfort in order to fulfill this great commission.

Regardless of what you hear from dubious sources, the largest groups of unsaved people are not in third-world countries, places without electricity or clean water and basic necessities. The largest population of unsaved are not in the diaspora around the world. The largest group of unreached adults for Jesus Christ are men right here in America. A staggering number of women leave their men at home on the couch or in the bed every week and attend church with no man by their side. It prompt us to ask the question, where are the men? Less than 40 percent of church attendees are men. They have become a missing commodity in society and especially in the sanctuaries. As the church progresses in its natural life cycles, men are extensively and peculiarly absent or unseen. Unsurprisingly, they are less likely to be a part of the leadership in the church. They are less likely to be greeters or ushers, serve in church axillaries or take part in crafting the vision for the future of the church. Even in the Catholic Church, in many parishes around the country, they have had to close churches because they cannot find enough men to enter the priesthood. Where are the brothers in our world?

It seems as if men are disconnected spiritually, leaving a void in our culture of kingdom men. There are many culprits for this desertion of men. Some are weakened and even neutered by abuse in the church and misinformation about what a kingdom man really is. Current pop culture has blurred the line of what a man is, and the church has been somewhat negligent to minister to the men who have disconnected from ministry work. As a result of this void, various areas of our culture are minus men and there is no true portrait of what a real kingdom man looks like.

Not only does the church need men, but the men also need the church. It is a give-and-take relationship. This is why God is sending out a clarion call for all real kingdom men to Man Up! This term means to accept responsibility and be the leader that God has called us to be.

I previously noted that a home without a man contributes to all kinds of social ills. The prisons wouldn't be as filled if men were in the homes. Jobs would not be left vacant if men were in the homes. When a man is not in the home, there is three times the probability that the family will live in poverty.

Men are needed in the church because they are a critical part of God's Kingdom Plan. The enemy has been extremely successful in removing men from the church because the enemy knows that when the man is missing, God's plan has a missing link. When we observe the history of the African-American church in particular, there were anointed men who led the people from their spiritual positions in the church and also spurred various movements toward social, economic and religious freedom. It's only in this current generation that we find the phenomenon of men missing in the church. Whenever the devil seeks to make a move on society, it is always against the men first. If the man is out of place, then the rest of the family will ultimately be displaced.

In Pharaoh's Egypt, under the fears of a takeover by the men of Israel, men were destroyed first. Under Herod, all of the male babies were killed in order to prevent what he perceived to be a takeover of his kingdom. Men need to be leading in the church because when that leadership is activated, other areas will become relevant and vibrant. I am not saying that a woman cannot lead and lead effectively. However, it's critical to note that there are some things that a woman can do but would not have to do if a strong, responsible man was in place.

One would criticize the church and say that the church is anti-man, because church is soft and appeals to the emotions only and men are not emotional creatures and so we would rather stay away. I can agree with the church touching emotions – it does – but I can't agree that this is the only area being ministered to. The power of the gospel of Christ should touch mind, soul and spirit. Furthermore, I disagree vehemently that men are unable to be emotional. Whenever I go to a New Orleans Saints game there are thousands upon thousands of men yelling, screaming and slapping high-fives with other men. I have seen men cry when a man loses in sport and it's OK, but the church is too emotional for a man? I can't buy that. The reality is that church for a man is like a prostate exam: it's uncomfortable and invasive, but it will save your life. The kingdom-minded man understands that his spirituality and the expression of emotions doesn't diminish the quality of his manhood, but rather strengthens his connection with his creator.

We have a society full of baby boys who are never able to grow into biblical manhood because they have not had a portrait of what a real kingdom man looks like. The implications of such a culture are seen in the many maladies in our society. Consider this: the majority of males grow up in a feminized world, but still have a warrior waiting to be unleashed inside of them. However, there is no one to unlock that genius on the inside of them or speak into their future and give them a hope to chase after. So those that attempt to develop into manhood must now portray manhood without ever seeing a genuine kingdom man lived out before them. Consequently, we have feminized males being portrayed in our culture and in our church. We have a philosophical bend in the culture towards woman who are forced to take roles that God never intended for a woman to have to fulfill. As a result, men are leaving their responsibilities to women to raise their sons and their daughters and now we have a generational disaster as the presence of manhood has totally been erased. It's past time for a new mentality among men to be presented in our churches. We can no longer give men a pass to be pathetic and duck their duties in the church. We need kingdom men to stand up.

Every man needs to be connected to the church because it's important that he has a spiritual covering. In the course of natural human progression, there is childhood, boyhood, adulthood, and prayerfully, manhood. As men progress through these first three stages, age is the stimulus and determining factor in which one reaches adulthood. This does not hold true for the stage of manhood. Manhood does not come because a male reaches a certain age; rather, manhood requires the acquiring of wisdom and taking on responsibilities. The interesting thing about each of these stages is that each is accompanied or preceded by a "hood." Due to the creative power and unique sensitivity and vulnerability of each stage, it is important that there is a hood attached to every stage of growth. A hood is something that covers or protects. A hood keeps the elements off. If you are in childhood, there are certain vulnerabilities that a child has and it is necessary that you have a responsible person to cover you: a parent. That's true at each stage of development. There is even a scholarly covering as well.

Once I attended the graduation of a friend who was receiving his PhD, and there was in this ceremony a conferring or hooding process that signifies that the graduate is covered with institutionally recognized knowledge. If a child who is going through childhood needs a covering and a student who is obtaining an advance degree needs a covering, then every man should have a covering to authenticate and validate his manhood. This is the kingdom order. In particular, every man should have a spiritual covering, or a pastor. There are no Lone Rangers in the kingdom of God. You cannot lead well unless you first submit to someone who serves as your hood. The man, according to the Bible, is the covering for the woman. It is very dangerous for a woman to submit to the covering of a man who has no covering himself. Women should require, before they give their hand in marriage, that her soon-to-be husband has a covering. This covering validates his manhood and speaks to his level of submission and humility to God's kingdom order.

Paul writes a letter to his spiritual son, Timothy, the senior pastor of the church at Ephesus, speaking to the importance of a maintaining the standards of God within the society. Timothy's submission to Paul demonstrates the necessity for even pastors to have a spiritual covering. The church at Ephesus had more importance than any of the other churches mentioned in the New Testament. When John wrote about the seven churches of Asia, the church at Ephesus was one of those seven – the epicenter of commerce, culture and a trend-setting city where everything that was in vogue took place, including idolatry. The Temple of Diana was located in Ephesus.

Part of the covering that Paul rendered to Timothy was in written communications. His letters to him were designed to teach him how things were supposed to go in the church of the Living God. The people of Ephesus understood architectural terms and language that Paul used in his letters for Ephesus. He saw the church as the "pillar and the ground of truth." The church was the place where real truth would be established and relied upon as a place of reference as things in the culture went wild. It was not in the plan of God for His Kingdom to look at the world to find its truth, but rather for the church to always be the source of truth and a standard-bearer for the world. Paul shares with Timothy that no matter how much the culture shifts or changes, the church must be the pillar and ground of truth for Kingdom believers. Paul was charging Timothy to preach and model this truth – the truth about God's order and the truth about God's expectations for the believer. Timothy submitted to the wisdom of his spiritual covering and found success for his life while living out the meaning of a true kingdom man. I am reminding every man that God's order is still the pillar and ground of truth in our modern culture. I thank God not just for my natural father, who is my hero and has taught me so much about being a man, but I also submit to and thank God for my pastor, my father in the ministry who serves as the spiritual covering for my ministry. There are many who mock this principle because those in the world cannot understand spiritual things. I must admit that I have not always agreed with nor was fond of many decisions that my pastor has made. However, I have never doubted the divine necessity of having a spiritual covering. This pillar of truth will always stand, despite what's going on in the culture.

There is a mission that God is sending the church on to reach and restore men back to their called place in the kingdom and in the culture, and it's founded on every man having a hood that covers him. A kingdom man who is spiritually minded and humbly submitted is a threat to the kingdom of darkness. We need kingdom men to arise and be an example to a generation in need. The church is responsible for producing kingdom men. ***A kingdom man is one that is to the family, what Christ is to the church***. Christ is the Savior of the church, and the man is to be the savior of the family! I conclude that the problem of our society is not simply politics, prejudice or poverty – these are symptoms of a larger problem, one that is paternal. **IF DAD DOESN'T COME HOME, THE BABY IS IN TROUBLE.** A cry has to go out for MEN to return to their place of leadership. If not, we are going to raise a generation of passive men, abusive men, effeminate men who produce after their own kind. We need the kingdom man to step up. We cannot lose this generation; we must make the shift!

Chapter 5

A Dominion **MEN**tality

Who's the Man?

I Chronicles 7:40 NKJV

40 All these were the children of Asher, heads of their fathers' houses, choice men, mighty men of valor, chief leaders. And they were recorded by genealogies among the army fit for battle; their number was twenty-six thousand.

Who's the Man?

This phrase came into play several years ago when comedian-turned-actor Martin Lawrence would ask that question to his girlfriend, Gina. The question, in and of itself, is profound because it becomes a question of identity in the times that we live. Contemporary culture has placed manhood under constant attack. As a result, we have essentially redefined manhood. The fact is that men have been called by God to lead. Again, this is no disrespect to women, but the call has been there since creation. Manhood is not just a position or title; it is a responsibility. Often men are led astray by what is shown of them in the media. Most of the portrayed images are fabricated to create a stereotypical depiction of that which is entertaining but not sustaining. Our boys and men are buying into every nuance of corruptive behavior, making those images the standard for manhood.

Some men can be described as "macho" men. They find their value in living by the sword, which means the probability is that they will die by the sword as well. This kind of image has created a myriad of men who embrace thuggery while housing pent-up anger and a criminal history that follows them everywhere they go. This man can do nothing for the women around them because he is regularly housed behind bars or has a short expected lifespan. His future lies in his imminent residence in a cemetery.

There are other men who would describe themselves as the "money man," one who sincerely believes that money makes the world go around. He is the one who is besieged with having to have a "hustle" in order to survive. I'm not referencing those who try to make ends meet by holding down several jobs at one time. That's a hard-working man, obsessed with trying to take care of his family. I'm talking about men who are looking for *easy* money with no work and instant reward. It does not matter what kind of hustle, as long as it generates cash that can be flashed.

There is nothing wrong with having money or a desire to be prosperous, but money sources can dry up. Money as your source of manhood is unstable at best and extremely volatile. What value is it to have a handful of dollars and still be unable to hold your family together? While there used to be a time when men were predominantly relied on to provide financially for the family, times have changed, and changed dramatically. Woman today in many regards are professionally and financially secure. So the role of a man solely to provide is no longer one that is desirable. A woman does not need a man whose purpose is to compete with her over who brings home the most money. Money should never define the strength of manhood. Every man should be leery of a woman who only loves him for his money. When you are really a man, a woman will willfully love and respect you because you provide more than just financial stability to the family.

There is yet another type of man called a "mommy man." These are males who can't get away from their momma long enough to please their wives. These men fail because they were simply the best man that mommy could make. They can't leave their mom's side long enough to invest in their own family. The Bible declares that a man should leave his mother and father and cleave to his wife. Leaving and cleaving is a vital part of growing into the man you are destined to be.

Finally, there is the mannish man. Everything is validated for him by how he is able to perform in the bedroom. He is the man as long as his sexuality can be sustained and validated by his bed partner. The question is whether he can get that same kind of validation in the boardroom and the classroom as he does from the bedroom. If you define yourself by the prowess of your bedroom actions, the reality is that it won't last forever. When that time has ended, there will still be the need for someone to complement that woman outside of the bedroom.

The real man is a kingdom man who has dominion. In the Book of Job, there is a portrait of a kingdom man. In those 42 chapters, you can see a man that went through a lot and when it was all over, he was still standing. He prevailed.

Job 29 reflects on a few things that took place in the midst of his personal history. It's in verse number two that we find the amazing attribute of Job as a kingdom man.

Job 29:2–5 NKJV

²*"Oh, that I were as in months past,*
As in the days when God watched over me;
³*When His lamp shone upon my head,*
And when by His light I walked through darkness;
⁴*Just as I was in the days of my prime,*
When the friendly counsel of God was over my tent;
⁵*When the Almighty was yet with me,*
When my children were around me;

A kingdom man has divine continuity. Job could reflect on his life and see that his entire life was due to the goodness of God. We need a generation who holds this attribute. With that divine continuity, God has favored and strengthened men. A real man realizes his limitations and knows that if it had not been for the Lord, he would not be where he is in life. He would be another statistic waiting for life to happen to him. There are so many times when I look over my life and point to times when it should have been over due to mistakes, misjudgments and plain carelessness, but the goodness of God's grace saw me through. We need men with a spiritual center who understand it is not about them! If God ever removed His Hand from me, I would be as a ship without a sail.

We are born males, but we must *become* men. Your anatomical structure dictates that fact. Based upon that principle, you can become an *old* male but never a real man. You don't become a man because there is hair on your chest or you become twenty-one years old. With some of the food that we are consuming, hair can come on your chest and face at thirteen. You become a man when you submit to the Lord and Savior, Jesus Christ. That is the genesis of your manhood.

It is the responsibility of the church to create a theo-centric worldview that places the entire earth under the Lordship of Jesus Christ. It is an obligation of the church to be the pillar of truth as to the definition of manhood. The societal culture wants us to look outward for the definition. The reality of truth is that your purpose is embedded within you through a connection with a Divine Center.

Every man is searching for *more* of God. In you, there is a God-size void that only He can fill. There is no substitute for the role that God is supposed to play in your life. You can, as the psalmist says in the lyrics:

"Searched all over
Couldn't find nobody
Looked high and low
Still couldn't find nobody…"

God designed *us* so that we might tap into *Him*. If you want to know the purpose of a created thing, you don't consult the creation; you consult the Creator. Therefore, there is no basis for looking outside for my purpose as a man; God formed me to be what He would have me become. When I connect with Divine Creation, I connect with both my destiny and my purpose.

It is difficult to describe the essence of Divine Connection, yet we can reflect on the psalmist David, who asked God not to take His Presence from him. You can lose a lot of things by which people identify you, but you are incomplete without God's Presence. You can lose wealth, position, and relationships that were dear to you. However, God can give you life when you should have qualified for death. To know that God is always in my corner rooting for me helps me through each day.

God has created us to have dominion. He put Adam in the garden and gave him authority and control. He was to keep it, cultivate it, and manage it so that it would keep on producing. He had dominion. God has given men that same kind of dominion. When we fail to handle dominion, we resort to domination. That is always a sign of insecurity and a lack of identity. You have dominion over your spouse, but you don't have a right to dominate her. You don't have to exercise your physical strength over your spouse. You can tell a person who is weak in dominion because he is always declaring that he is "the boss" or "in charge." People who continually remind you of their title probably don't have the *real* authority behind that title. If you are in charge, everybody over whom you are in charge will know it without your saying it every fifteen minutes.

You need to consider becoming a "dominionaire." As a dominionaire, you learn how to be creative. You know how to cultivate. God gives you everything in seed form that you might as the "dominionaire" cause it to produce, replenish, and multiply.

Asher, in this text, is translated "happy." He was special because of the heritage that he built through his children. He had five children. We can find out much about the kind of man he was by what he produced in his children. He was a man who knew what it was like to create, cultivate, and to keep.

From his five children, he created an army of 26,000 men of valor. They were heads of their father's house. Asher raised "lead men" and not "follow men." Your leadership effectiveness is based on the atmosphere that you create for others to flourish. Good leaders create the right climate for fellowship and development. A leader has a picture or vision of what the outcome is going to look like. He sees out in front of everybody else things that become obvious to others later. A leader has a clear mental picture of the future. A man without a vision should not become a "partner" with anyone else. Women might need to ask their potential mate about his vision of his future before she embraces a more substantive relationship. Without vision, people perish. A visionary does not just see an acorn; he sees an oak tree.

Without vision, all you can see is right now. All you can see is the acorn season of your life. You can become consumed by what is currently presented as your future reality. It may not be that at all. Caleb and Joshua had a vision of the land they spied that was consistent with what God said was in store for Israel. Although all the other spies saw the inhabitants of the Promised Land as giants and themselves as grasshoppers, Caleb and Joshua saw the Promise of God as their reality. They saw themselves handling it.

Vision can allow you to survive your tough times. There may be *days* of suffering that you are enduring right now, but God will give you years of sunshine, triumph and victory. What is your vision?

Chapter 6

A Persistent **MEN**tality:

See It Through

1 Corinthians 9:24-27 NKJV

24 Do you not know that those who run in a race all run, but one receives the prize? Run in such a way that you may obtain it. 25 And everyone who competes for the prize is temperate in all things. Now they do it to obtain a perishable crown, but we for an imperishable crown. 26 Therefore I run thus: not with uncertainty. Thus I fight: not as one who beats the air. 27 But I discipline my body and bring it into subjection, lest, when I have preached to others, I myself should become disqualified.

Hebrews 12:1-2 AMP

12 Therefore then, since we are surrounded by so great a cloud of witnesses [who have borne testimony to the Truth], let us strip off and throw aside every encumbrance (unnecessary weight) and that sin which so readily (deftly and cleverly) clings to and entangles us, and let us run with patient endurance and steady and active persistence the appointed course of the race that is set before us,

2 Looking away [from all that will distract] to Jesus, Who is the Leader and the Source of our faith [giving the first incentive for our belief] and is also its Finisher [bringing it to maturity and perfection]. He, for the joy [of obtaining the prize] that was set before Him, endured the cross, despising and ignoring the shame, and is now seated at the right hand of the throne of God.

Life is just like a race that runners run. The truth of the matter is that you have to prepare and you must be focused on your life's journey. Everyone wants to win in life, but most people don't. Most people settle for their lot and never reach the goals that God has outlined for their life. So consequently, dreams and goals stay on the shelf and we waddle in average and mediocrity our entire lives.

I am surprised at the number of people who come to me excited and inspired about a goal that God has given them to start a business, to go back to school or to rededicate themselves to Christian living, yet when the storms and winds of life blow and they must persevere, they throw in the towel. What many of these individuals are lacking is a spirit of persistency. It's during times of testing that you must learn to be persistent.

American history is replete with individuals who had to persevere in order to see their dreams come true. Many of us who are history enthusiasts have heard and read about the often-repeated story and legacy of our sixteenth president, Abraham Lincoln. We know the history of his unparalleled leadership and courage in the Civil War and the Emancipation Proclamation and even his monument that now stands on the Washington Mall. We are familiar with what he represents as a symbol to our nation and as a testament to the democracy we say we stand for. However, little is told about what Mr. Lincoln had to endure and overcome for him to be seen as the champion that we now revere him as.

President Lincoln's Trials Are Legendary:

- He had trouble with in-laws who thought he was too poor to marry his wife.
- He had four children of which only one lived until adulthood.
- In 1832 he failed in business and was denied entry into law school.
- In 1835 he was engaged and his fiancé died.
- In 1836 he had a nervous breakdown and suffered from depression.
- In 1836 he was defeated for speaker of the house.
- In 1843 he was defeated for nomination to congress.
- In 1849 he was rejected for Land Officer.
- In 1854 he was defeated for U.S. Senate.
- In 1856 he was defeated for vice presidential nomination.
- In 1858 he was defeated for U.S. Senate again.
- In 1860 he was elected president.

Most would have given up and determined that success, especially in politics, was too evasive and not God's will for their lives. However, the question must be asked, how did Mr. Lincoln continue amidst all the failures, shame and disgrace that he consistently experienced in his life? Certainly as he endured each trial, he wrestled with the thoughts that God couldn't have made him a champion. I believe that Abraham Lincoln survived every season of his life because he embodied the spirit of persistency.

There is no such thing as an undefeated champion. There isn't a champion that has not tasked defeat in some areas of life. If we are going to win, we must win despite our circumstances and not simply because of them. We all have experienced defeat and failure, we have experienced some closed doors, we have experienced relationships that have failed, we have experienced sickness in our body, and God is saying you are still a champion because champions are not champions because of how well they win, but how well they recover from their losses in their life. Champions are determined by how well you bounce back when you experience defeat. It doesn't matter how much you fast, how hard you pray, or how often you attend church: life happens to everyone. It's not what happens to you but what happens after life hits you that determines the pedigree of your mentality. There is going to be stuff that goes awry in your marriage, in your relationships, and in your career that's going to teach you perseverance. What you are going through right now is just tuition; it's a down-payment for what God is going to produce and birth in your future.

We all must pull on the power of persistency in order to win in life. Just because you have been destined to WIN this year does not mean you won't have to deal with and overcome and manage yourself in the midst of defeat.

The true test for any champion is not how well they win, but how they recover from a loss. What is your goal? To be a better Christian? To defeat bad habits? To pull your family or perhaps your career together?

If you don't have the ability to be persistent, you will never walk in victory. Life's events happen to us all, but the question is how you will respond and how you will deal with it.

PERSISTENCE is an attitude and strong desire to continue on a course even in the face of difficulty.

What goals have God given you this year? Be persistent, desire to be all that God wants you to be in life and continue to bear up under pressure. You have the ability on the inside of you to continue. There are two things you might do when things get tight: either you are going to fight, or you are going to take flight. You must fight, fight, fight! Giving up is not the answer; you must stand still and fight to receive the promises of God.

There is a danger of quitting too soon. You don't know you are closer now than you have ever been to your breakthrough and your release. This is not quitting time, but pressing time. You must press your way through.

Hebrews 12:1-2 AMP

12 Therefore then, since we are surrounded by so great a cloud of witnesses [who have borne testimony to the Truth], let us strip off and throw aside every encumbrance (unnecessary weight) and that sin which so readily (deftly and cleverly) clings to and entangles us, and let us run with patient endurance and steady and active persistence the appointed course of the race that is set before us,...

We must live the life that has been set before us. Free yourself from the burdens and stresses in life, and live. God wants you to live a life that's happy, rewarding and joyful because this is the race you must run.

How Do I Continue When In a Hard Place?

LOOK TO CHAMPIONS

Every person who is a champion had to fight some battles to win. The writer of Hebrews lets us know that in this race called life, we have some witnesses that will testify if we need evidence that you can win! They are not spectators, but they are witnesses.

They will speak from their life experience and encourage you to simply continue to hold fast to the promises of God. God places these individuals in your life to declare that we overcome by the blood of the lamb and the word of the testimony. Their lives are witnesses to us to let us know the faithfulness of God. If you have family problems, let Joseph testify. Joseph had issues with his own brothers, but Joseph can testify that what the devil meant for evil, God will work it out for your good. If you are overwhelmed on your job, let Moses testify. Moses had the enormous task of leading God's people and he wanted to quit and give up, but Moses can testify that when your heart is overwhelmed, you can lean on a rock that is higher than you. If you have haters and enemies all around you, let David testify. David can testify, "No weapon formed against you will be able to prosper and every tongue that rises in judgment will be condemned." If you feel as though you are being falsely crucified, let Jesus testify that God will raise you up from every grave that the enemy has dug for you.

We must have a righteous role model that encourages us and comforts us in our race. They will testify that God will give you another chance and that it's not over until God says it's over. We must look to champions!

LOOK AT YOURSELF.

When we have failures in life, we must not blame people or things. We must look at the man in the mirror and ask him to change his ways. Many times our ability to continue is based on the adjustments that we are willing to make. A winning athlete will always have to choose between what he is willing to lay aside, sacrifice, give up. In order to go up, we must be willing to give up.

We must understand that we have weights and we have sin. The weights are not the sin, but the weights can lead to the sin. The weights are any habits or impediments that stop us from running full-speed ahead. Weights are things that distract you while you are running your race. When I was in high school I played football. On Fridays we used to wear ankle weights and walk around school and you knew who was on the football team because that was our little fad, wearing the weights. The ankle weights would strengthen us for the game; however, we could never wear them in the game because they would have slowed down our performance. If you are going to do your best in life, you will have to get rid of the weighs. Weights can be hangouts, people and time-killers. If you want to continue and win, you must lose the weights. Your weights may be your past failures. When we are facing failures of any kind, we have three options: We can frame our failures, we can blame our failures or we can learn from them and bury them. Champions are able to lose the weights! If you want to experience victory, you must lay the weights aside.

LOOK AT JESUS.

Jesus is the author and the finisher of our faith. Jesus is where it begins and ends. Make sure you put your faith in the right place. Whatever you are presently dealing with, when it seems overwhelming and you feel like you want to give up and quit, consider Jesus, because everything he was, we are. We must trust that God will give us the grace we need for the battle we are fighting. We can't get into tight situations and take our eyes off of Jesus. He has to be our focus. You must put all distractions aside and focus on the spiritual side of this thing.

Enduring the cross doesn't mean that I'm going to tolerate the cross, it means that I'm going to get educated by the cross. In every adversity and seemingly failing event in your life is the seed of success, but as champions we must expect the cross and endure the cross. We must be educated by the cross.

What determines the strength of our persistency is the value we place on the goal. We will see how bad you want something based on what you are willing to go through to attain it. Jesus wanted us to experience victory so bad that He endured what it took to get us free. You can last because you are focused on Jesus. His wisdom, his power and his direction become yours! The most persistent person we know is God...He never gives up on us and we should never give up on what He said we could do.

Don't Let Discouragement Discourage You!

1 Kings 19:1-6 NKJV

19 And Ahab told Jezebel all that Elijah had done, also how he had executed all the prophets with the sword. 2 Then Jezebel sent a messenger to Elijah, saying, "So let the gods do to me, and more also, if I do not make your life as the life of one of them by tomorrow about this time." 3 And when he saw that, he arose and ran for his life, and went to Beersheba, which belongs to Judah, and left his servant there.

4 But he himself went a day's journey into the wilderness, and came and sat down under a broom tree. And he prayed that he might die, and said, "It is enough! Now, Lord, take my life, for I am no better than my fathers!"

5 Then as he lay and slept under a broom tree, suddenly an angel[a] touched him, and said to him, "Arise and eat." 6 Then he looked, and there by his head was a cake baked on coals, and a jar of water. So he ate and drank, and lay down again.

If you are going to be successful at any endeavor in your life, no matter what it is – your God-given assignment or perhaps your professional career, your ambitions or your dreams – you must first master the desire to quit. In between starting something and finishing something, you will have to wrestle with the desire to quit. Don't think it strange, because this feeling of quitting has surfaced in every life. Quitting is one of those things that we all will have to wrestle with. Anyone that has been called to do something significant will always feel like quitting before they reach their God-ordained destiny.

You must understand that you are never celebrated or applauded for what you started in life. No, you are only rewarded by God for what you finish. Nobody gets a gold medal or a blue ribbon because they started the race. It's only for those things that you finish in life that you get celebrated or rewarded. I have never had an opportunity to run in a marathon; however, several friends of mine have. They tell me that when running in a marathon, the runner hits this place on about the thirteenth mile that they call the wall; it's when everything in your physical body is telling you to shut it down, and it is during that time that you must press your way past this wall in order to finish the race. Now the interesting thing about a marathon is that nobody ever knows who wins a marathon, because the goal of the marathon is not to win but to FINISH. Life is just like a marathon. Life will throw a wall at you, life will hand you some setbacks, life will throw failure your way, and it's at that time that you must not quit.

It's just like an athlete who starts off in a marathon: as they get near the finish line, the desire to quit kicks in. That's just how it is in our lives. The devil always tries to put pressure on you both mentally and physically to quit. This is why it's so important that you pray that God will give you a "finisher's spirit." Everywhere you go, you must declare in the atmosphere that you are not a quitter but a finisher.

If the truth were told, there are some things this year that you started out believing God for, but now that some time has passed, you are saying, "Lord, I don't know anymore." It's so alarming, the number of people each year that get married and at the ceremony they stand before the pastor, family and friends in the Presence of the Lord and say, "I do," and 36 months later, are saying in the same breath, "I DON'T want it anymore." Just walking away, quitting what they wanted and later regretted. Starting a thing is the easy part, but finishing a thing is the challenging part. You can't quit if you experience setback or failure; it will lead you to **DISAPPOINTMENT, DISCOURAGEMENT** and **DESIRE TO QUIT**.

DISAPPOINTMENT is when God or people don't do what you thought they could, when you thought they should, how you thought they would.

The only area of disappointment in life is with people and God. It's interesting because disappointment can stem from a lot of areas in our lives. To be discouraged means your enthusiasm for a thing has diminished. It's when you have no more passion. Disappointment leads to discouragement and discouragement leads to quitting. The adversity, discouragement, and disappointment can stem from a lot of things in your life. Disappointment can stem from goal achievement: You may have initially set out some goals you desired to reach that have yet to come to pass. Another area is relationship goals; perhaps a relationship dissolved, or maybe there was some drama in a relationship, or you experienced a separation or divorce or the loss of a loved one that you hadn't finished loving yet. A third area is your career or calling, because of the weight of calling that's on your life. See, as Christians, we don't necessarily have careers but we have callings; we have stuff that we were created to do. You can be created to inspire, to encourage, to educate or care for the sick. There is a burden that goes along with every calling, and there is a weight that goes along with every career. In addition, self can cause you to have the desire to quit. We all can be honest that there have been times when we were disappointed in ourselves. There are times you must speak to yourself. Sometimes the person you need to check is yourself. In these times, you must speak directly to yourself and say, "You've got to get yourself together, man. You're still going in cycles like this. You're still allowing them to get under your skin." Last, we can get disappointed with God. This isn't something that we would freely and willfully admit, but inwardly we may have a problem with God because we feel that God has let us down or disappointed us. We all are guilty of failing some test. We all have by now moments: "By now, God, you should have done this." Whatever the issue may be, we must recognize that in in order to overcome quitting, we must have resilience. Resilience is the capacity to bounce back from adversity, discouragement, or disappointment. Now let's be honest: resilience won't stop disappointment from entering your life, but resilience will cause you to bounce back. You can't quit because you are resistant. The thing that makes a ball that's thrown to the ground bounce back is not what name is on the ball, but what's on the inside. Successful people are not folks who don't hit the bottom; they're people who hit the bottom but bounce back. I want to encourage you to bounce back from every adversity and disappointment that hits your life. You can't quit, because you are about to bounce back. You possess too much Holy Ghost in you for your life to go flat. It's not over for you. You will survive every attack of the enemy.

It's time to bounce back and pick up your head. God has not created you to die right where you are. It's the ability to get your balance after you have been knocked off-course.

If you have failed in life, failure is only failure if when you hit bottom you stay there and don't bounce back. If you bounce back, it's not failure, it's tuition. It's what you had to pay or learn in order to get to where you are. If you look closely at the life of any person that has had any measure of success, I can show you a person who had to bounce back, had to exemplify resilience, had to pay tuition. God is not going to allow you to stay down.

Let's look at a fella who quit: Elijah. Elijah helps us understand what it's like to quit. He quit the ministry, gave up, said he had enough. Elijah was being threatened by an evil spirit, Jezebel. He ran for his life because of fear of this spirit. Jezebel is a controlling spirit that comes to intimidate you. This type of spirit has to control everything and this spirit leads to manipulation.

The question is, how did Elijah get to this point or place of wanting to quit? The truth of the matter is, you can be at the height of your career or life and want to quit.

How Did Elijah Get to the Point of Quitting?

Elijah set unrealistic goals and expectations. Unrealistic expectations can cause you to quit. Elijah thought he had it all figured out. He was so comfortable in the way things had always been that he never fathomed that things could change. Elijah was a powerful man of God whom God used to prophesy the release and the stopping of rain during a season of drought. Elijah was God's man-servant. Wherever God told Elijah to go, he obeyed. When God told him to go to the brook and a raven was going to feed him there, Elijah did it. When the brook dried up and God told him to go to a widow woman's house and she would provide for him, Elijah obeyed. Elijah was an obedient man of God.

One day Elijah had a meeting at Mount Caramel with the prophets of Baal and he challenged the prophets of Baal to call on their God to rain down fire. Elijah was testing the authenticity and power of the god they worshiped. The prophets of Baal called on their god and Elijah called on his God. The expectation was that once the prophets of Baal witnessed the power of Elijah's God, they would be converted. However, that was not the conclusion of the matter. Once the battle was won by the God of Elijah, Ahab and Jezebel became angered and breathed threats to murder Elijah. Elijah had false expectations in that his achievement would result in celebration, but instead he got intimidating threats.

Misguided expectations are ones that we orchestrate in our minds but that didn't come from God. We anticipated the end results to be one thing, but God never promised us that particular end result. When you have unrealistic expectations, you will always be disappointed, experience discouragement and failure. Carefully examine your life and ask yourself these realistic questions. Are you expecting someone in your life to do what only God can do in your life? To fulfill you in some way that only God can fulfill you?

Unmanaged Emotions Can Cause You to Quit.

Elijah was plagued with so many evil spirits. He was dealing with fear, rejection, and suicide. If you don't manage these emotions, they will eventually turn into bad thoughts, and bad thoughts turn into bad decisions. Elijah allowed his negative emotions to control his life. Whatever you do, don't let your emotions be your instructions.

Don't make emotional decisions; decide to take a cool-down time to really assess your situation. Emotional decisions often are erroneous decisions. You must get to the point that you balance your emotions: where you don't get too excited and you don't get too far down. Simply manage your emotions by taking the time to respond and not overreact.

Unbalanced Isolation Can Cause You to Quit.

1 Kings 19:3 NKJV

3 And when he saw that, he arose and ran for his life, and went to Beersheba, which belongs to Judah, and left his servant there.

Hebrews 10:25 NKJV

25 not forsaking the assembling of ourselves together, as is the manner of some, but exhorting one another, and so much the more as you see the Day approaching.

Elijah was doing life at this point by himself. It's not a good idea to isolate yourself, because if the devil can get you alone, isolated and off by yourself, you won't have anyone to encourage you. God never intended for it to be just you, Jesus and the word. You need to surround yourself with other Christian like-minded brothers.

Don't leave your encouragement, your help, when you are experiencing adversity. Connect with the people who are around you to keep you strengthened and encouraged. Elijah lost the strength and the encouragement of the prayers and fellowship of others. There are so many reasons we isolate ourselves, such as embarrassment, self-pity, pride and jealousy. This is the trick of the devil, to get you alone so that he can torment your mind with negative thinking. Sooner or later life will catch up with you and you will experience burnout and have no one to share life with. Don't allow this to be your ending. Ask God to send you covenant brothers you can connect with that can help you bear your burden.

Unwise Comparison Can Cause You to Quit.

Elijah started comparing where he was to where he thought he would be. Elijah made the mistake we all do from time to time, and that is comparing himself to others who did what he was doing.

Comparisons kill us. It's dangerous to compare ourselves because we can never win. You can only run your race.

You must be comfortable in who God created you to be. You have your own uniqueness. When you copy, the best you can be is a copy. Be You.

When you decide to do you, it's going to be easy. It's stressful being someone else and you will always quit.

The good news is that when you are at your lowest point, an angel will come to you to encourage you. You can't quit now because your angel is on the way. God sends angels to strengthen you and to encourage you. Angel comes to confirm some things. When Jesus was in the wilderness, the Lord sent angels to encourage them.

Angels come to:

- *STRENGTHEN YOU*
- *ENCOURAGE YOU*
- *PROTECT YOU*

You can't quit because God has an angel specifically assigned to you. Be patient, because your angel is on the way. You've come too far to give up now. This is your time and season to embrace and move forward with **A CHAMPION MENtality.** God is doing a new thing in you. Old things have passed away; behold, **ALL THINGS** have become new.

About the Author

Dennis R. Hebert, Jr. was born in Los Angeles, California on November 30, 1977 to Reverend and Mrs. Dennis R. Hebert, Sr. He was reared in Baton Rouge, Louisiana and later relocated to New Orleans, Louisiana where he married Tranecia Williams and is the proud father of three sons Dennis III., Dylan, and Drake Hebert.

Dennis R. Hebert, Jr. attended Nicholls State University in Thibodaux, LA and is a graduate of the University of Louisiana at Monroe (1999). He is a former President of the ULM College Chapter of the NAACP, where he began his leadership development by organizing *"Get Out to Vote"* campaigns, voter awareness drives, and was instrumental in starting the collegiate chapter. Elder Hebert's commitment and passion for the word of God motivated him to pursue his theological training at the Darryl S. Brister Bible College and Theological Seminary in New Orleans, Louisiana where he studied Pastoral Studies. He is presently pursuing a Master of Divinity at United Theological Seminary, Dayton, Ohio.

On December 18, 2005 Pastor Dennis R. Hebert Jr. was installed as the Senior Pastor of the Beacon Light Baptist Church of Hammond where under his leadership the membership has grown from 300 members to over 1600 members and growing in just six short years. Pastor Hebert has a unique and passionate approach for teaching and preaching God's word. Complimenting his passion for the word of God is his tireless commitment for effective and relevant community outreach. Pastor Hebert has championed the cause of education and empowerment within Beacon Light and the greater Hammond community.

Beacon Light under Pastor Hebert's leadership has instituted a city-wide after school tutoring program to bridge the gap in education, a summer educational enrichment program to keep students engaged in learning through the summer months, and an annual HIV/AIDS awareness program to educate the community of prevention and treatments of this disease.

He is the president and founder of Dennis R. Hebert Ministries (DRH Ministries), an organization designed to empower and develop men and women spiritually, educationally, and economically. DRH Ministries awards annual Leaders of Tomorrow Scholarships to deserving college students within the Hammond community. In addition, the ministry focuses on impacting the lives of teenagers through a "Welcome to Manhood" outreach for teen boys and "Diva Society" outreach for teen girls. These outreach programs are designed to prepare our teens for the rigors of the real world and to provide role models and spiritual guidance as they transition into adulthood.

Pastor Hebert also serves as General Secretary for Beacon Light International Ministries, the governing body and he is a member of the Board of Directors for the Beacon Light Foundation of Hammond, Restoration Pregnancy Resource Center in Hammond, former member of the Hammond Chamber of Commerce. Pastor Hebert was installed on Sunday, August 18, 2013 as the General Overseer of Protocol for the Full Gospel Baptist Church Fellowship International. He is actively involved in the Hammond Community and takes very seriously his calling to impact the culture for Christ. With all that God continues to do, Pastor Hebert is committed to remaining a humble servant of God used for His Glory.

Dennis R. Hebert Ministries

Dennis R. Hebert Ministries is a non-profit organization empowering men and women to fulfill purpose and reach their destiny. Our mission is to become an oasis of hope in the community by promoting and providing outreach programs with an intentional emphasis on:

- Education
- Life-Skills
- Leadership and
- Spiritual Empowerment.

DRH Ministries initiatives include **Leaders of Tomorrow Scholarship** program established to award deserving college students with funds to help supplement the financial obligations of higher education, **Welcome to Manhood / Diva Society** is designed to educate, instruct, empower and expose young men and women on the HOW-TO's of fulfilling their visions and dreams and **Elev8 Lunch Club** targets junior high and high school students to provide various mentoring opportunities by mature, gifted and role model men and women in the community. DRH Ministries will also leverage the preaching and teaching of the gospel of Jesus Christ to empower individuals to overcome life circumstances and to live a victorious life by providing sermon CDs, DVDs, books and other means of media such as podcast, Live Video streaming and several social media platforms.

Dennis R. Hebert, Jr.

Please connect with the ministry by visiting our website at DRHMinistries.org and stay up to date with everything we are doing via social media on Facebook, DRHMinistries, Instagram, @DennisRHebertJr and Twitter @DennisHebertJr. Subscribe to our Podcast on iTunes or Podbean.